The
Wedding
Covenant

Birth in Love

Phillip A. Baker

Table of Contents

Dedication

Acknowledgement
Introduction
Giving of the Bride
Prayer
Exhortation to the Groom and Bride
The Contrast between a Covenant and a Contract
Profession of Your Love

Presentation of the Rings

Pronouncement
The LORD's Table

Oneness at the Fellowship Meal

Blessing of the Union

Unity Candle Lighting

Presentation to the Congregation

Creating Love

About the Author

Dedication

To my beautiful wife, Marva, you are truly my treasure and gift from God! Thank you for your love and inspiration, for always

nudging me to fulfill my God-given potential!
For your strength, patience and prayers which enabled me to keep moving forward.

Acknowledgement

To Robyn Norwood, I appreciate your labor of love in assisting me with the completion of this project.

Introduction

God said, "it's not good for man to be alone; I will make him a helper, a companion. GOD put the Man into a deep sleep. As he slept he removed one of his ribs and replaced it with flesh. GOD then used the rib that he had taken from the Man to make Woman and presented her to the Man." **Genesis 2:18, 21-22 MSG**

Adam opened his eyes and looked up. And WOW! He saw the most beautiful being of all God's creation. This is the one! Flesh of my flesh and bone of my bone!

It was love at first sight!

Clasping hands, they walked off together under the smiling approval of their Creator's love.

One of God's primary purposes in marriage was for two people, male and female, to be joined together as one in Love and mutual harmony-- Two hearts laid upon the altar that are ablaze with the fire of Divine love, here to be fused into one sacred instrument for God, becoming stronger, more efficient, more durable than one alone could ever be!

This was a deliberate and gracious design of the Divine architect of the marriage covenant whereby the man and woman would be united, not only legally, but totally.
It's the oldest union known to man, a beautiful reflection of the love between the Father, Son, and Holy Spirit.

This book was written to be used in the consolidation in seamless oneness two organic individuals created in the image and likeness of God, therefore what God has joined together, let no one desecrate it by dividing them!

The Wedding Covenant

Birth in Love

Giving of the Bride

To the Father: Who gives this woman's hand in marriage?

Response: I do.

To the Congregation: Is there anyone present who knows of any reason why this couple should not be married?

MAY THEY SPEAK NOW OR FOREVER BE SILENT.

To the Groom: Take your bride's hand and step forward, please.

Prayer

To the Congregation: Please remain standing as we agree as "one" in the LORD in prayer.

Gracious Father, we come together as "one" in the beauty of Holiness, to witness Your Grace and Love in action.

Joining together in seamless "oneness" two organic individuals created in Your image and likeness.

It was of Your choosing and Your doing that You decided to manifest Yourself in flesh and blood.

As You join them together, cause them to give a tangible expression of Your wonderful kindness and love for all to see and embrace Your love in Jesus' Name! Amen!

To the Congregation: You may be seated.

Exhortation to the Groom & Bride

To the Groom & Bride: Marriage is the oldest union known to man. It's a beautiful reflection of the love between the Father, Son, and Spirit. It dates back to Creation in the Garden of Eden where God Himself performed the first marriage ceremony and gave away the first bride.

It is the joyous act of uniting a man and woman in the most intimate of human relationships for life; a sharing of experience and adventure where mutual understanding has blossomed into love.

It's established by God as a covenant and not a contract, by which the parties embark upon a life together in mutual affection and devotion, till death shall separate them.

The Contrast Between a Covenant and a Contract

- A covenant is based on trust.

  A contract is based on distrust.

- A covenant is based on limitless, yet selfless obligations.
  A contract is based on limited liability.

- A covenant can't be broken if a new incident occurs.
  A contract can be annulled by mutual agreement.

Wife: I exhort you to be good to your husband and responsive to his needs. Cultivate inner beauty-- the gentle, gracious kind God delights in. Understand and support him in ways that show your support for Christ.
The husband provides love and leadership to his wife the way Christ does to His church-- not by dominating, but by cherishing.

So just as the church submits to Christ as He exercises such love and leadership, wives should likewise submit to their husbands.

Husband: I exhort you to go all out in your love for your wife, exactly as Christ did for the church—a love marked by giving, <u>not getting</u>. Christ's love makes the church whole. His words evoke her beauty. Everything he does and says is designed to bring the best out of her, dressing her in dazzling white silk, radiant with holiness.

And that is how husbands ought to love their wives. They're really doing themselves a favor— since they're already "one" in marriage.

A man could go through many disciplines in life to make himself look good financially or even go to great expense to win the applause of others. He could diligently workout in the gym and trim his body to perfection, <u>but the most valuable thing he can do to himself is to love his wife</u>.
No one abuses his own body, does he? No, he feeds and pampers it. That's how Christ treats us (the church) since we are part of His body.

And this is why a man should separate himself from his own parents to be glued to his wife. No longer, two separate people, they become "one flesh." {They are now merged into "<u>one new identity</u>"}.

The secret of a successful marriage is reflected in this inseparable union between Christ and the church, as God's redeemed image and likeness in man. (This union ultimately defines both marriage and church).

In conclusion then, no one has any excuse to love his wife less than what he loves himself; at the same time every wife is now free and fully empowered to honor her husband in the same context and devotion as the church would respond to the love initiative of Christ. Ephesians 5:32,33 MB *(We love him because he first loved us! [1 John 4: 19])*

Sum & Substance: Marriage is a portrait of mutually yielding to one another. It celebrates love's initiative, whether coming from the husband or the wife. This awakens a different level of commitment beyond any sense of duty or guilt. Inspired by the selfless consideration you witnessed in Christ, show perfect courtesy to one another. Scripture declares that **a man's wife is his treasure, she is a gift from God!**

So as Christ restored the church to Himself in His radiant image and likeness; without any distraction of blemished past; no wrinkle or scar of sin's abuse remains; she stands before Him in immaculate innocence, with no sense of inferiority, suspicion, blame, regret or pressure to perform. This is how you should receive each other. This will put separation and divorce out of business! {Francois Du Toit}

To the Family and Friends: You are not here out of tradition, but as witnesses, and to cheer on this precious union. <u>This is their moment</u>. Your part is to encourage and support them in your love and prayers. And regardless of what circumstances that may arise, see to it that they remain secure in Grace, Peace & Love!

Profession of Your Love

To The Groom: ____________________, do you take __________________, as your wife, going all out in your love for her, exactly as Christ did for the church-- to cherish and pamper her <u>unconditionally</u> as your own flesh for the rest of you lives?

Groom's Response: I do!

Turn to Her and Make this Profession of Love:

I __________________, according to the Word of God: leave my father and mother and I join myself to you to be a husband to you __________________, from this moment forward we are now merged into "<u>one new identity</u>".

To The Bride: _______________________, do you take
_______________________, as your husband responsive to his needs, understand and support him <u>unconditionally</u> in ways that show your support for Christ for the rest of your lives?

Bride's Response: I do!

Turn to Him and Make this Profession of Love:
I _______________________, according to the word of God: Submit myself to be a wife to you _______________________, honoring your leadership and embracing your love. From this moment forward we are now merged into "<u>one new identity</u>."

Presentation of the Rings

To the Groom: <u>May I have the Bride's ring, please</u>?
The ring symbolizes the transfer of authority, strength, resources, and protection.
Ring: Heb-prim root, to sink down; fasten, settle, seal or for sealing.
Scripture Reference: The Law of First Mention- "The Law of First Mention" simply means that the very first time any important word is mentioned in the Bible [usually, of course, is in Genesis, the first book of the Bible]. Scripture gives that word its most complete, and accurate, meaning to not only serve as a "key" in understanding the word's Biblical concept, but to also provide a foundation for its fuller development in later parts of the Bible.

[And Pharaoh said, "I hereby put you <u>in charge of the entire land of Egypt</u>." Then Pharaoh placed his own signet ring on Joseph's finger as <u>a symbol of authority</u>. Gen. 41:41,42 NLT]. [Now go ahead and send a message to the Jews in the king's name, telling them whatever you want, and <u>seal</u> it with the king's signet ring. But remember that whatever has already been written in the king's name and sealed with his signet ring <u>can never be revoked</u>." Est.8:8 NLT].

In a Covenant relationship, the ring symbolizes <u>identification</u>.
Scripture Declares: You should honor and delight in each other....in this new life of God's grace, you're equal. So treat her as your equal!

To the Groom: Take this ring, place it on her finger and say to her: "With this ring, I thee wed. It is a symbol of my love for you. By God's grace, I will provide emotional and physical support, including all the resources afforded me by our Heavenly Father. I will be strong, loving, considerate, respectful, faithful and understanding of you in Jesus' Name!

To the Bride: <u>May I have the Groom's ring, please</u>?

To the Bride: Take this ring, place it on his finger and say to him: "With this ring I thee wed. It is a symbol of my love for you. By God's grace, I will provide emotional and physical support, including all the resources afforded me by our Heavenly Father. I will be strong, loving, considerate, respectful, faithful and understanding of you in Jesus' Name!

Pronouncement

To the Groom and Bride: Join hands, please.

You have both proclaimed your love for each other before God and these witnesses. You have agreed to share your lives together, recognizing each other as equal in this life of grace.

Therefore, as a representative of Jesus Christ, before The Almighty God. In the Name of The Father, Son and by the Power of The Holy Spirit. I now pronounce you "One" husband and wife!

You may now Salute your Bride!

The LORD's Table

The Blood Covenant or **The LORD'S Table**--we typically call it *Communion*, is based on the
oldest covenant known to mankind.

It evidently began in the Garden of Eden. **{Unto Adam also and to his wife did the LORD God make coats of skin and clothed them}. Genesis 3:21 KJ**

Scripture shows evidence that God entered into covenant with Adam at the beginning of time, when Adam violated God's command.
[Blood was poured out to cover Adam's guilt].

The word Covenant means **"to cut."** The idea is an incision where blood flows.

So almost everywhere we see the word Covenant in Scripture, it indicates **"to cut the Covenant."**

The entire Redemptive plan of God is hinged on the two Covenants - The old and the new.

Oneness at The Fellowship Meal

1 Corinthians 11:18, 23-26 MIRROR BIBLE My priority concern is that you are divided into different and distracting opinions when you gather as a church. Our focus is the nitty-gritty essence of the gospel. I believe in oneness, not divisions.

The two of you are now merged into one new identity! When you agree on anything, based on the finished work of the Christ, you can expect it to come to pass for you.

11:23 Let me remind you then what we are actually celebrating in our fellowship meal: The night in which the Lord Jesus was betrayed, he took bread.
11:24 and gave thanks; breaking the bread into portions, he said, "Realize your association with my death, every time you eat, remember my body that was broken for you!"

Give the Bread to the Couple: You may eat.

11:25 He did exactly the same with the cup after supper and said, "This cup holds the wine of the new covenant in my blood; you celebrate me every time you drink with this understanding!" (From now on our meals are meaningful. We celebrate the fact that the incarnation reveals our redemption; the promise became a person. He redeemed our original value, identity, and innocence; he died our death and defines the life we now live).

Give the Cup to the Couple: You may drink.

11:26 Your every meal makes the mandate of his coming relevant and communicates the meaning of the new covenant. *(Whether you eat or drink, you are declaring your joint inclusion in his death and resurrection, confirming your redeemed innocence).*

Blessing of the Union

Galatians 3:13 MB Says: Christ redeemed us from the curse as a consequence of our failure to keep the law. In His cross, He concentrated the total curse of the human race upon himself. In His abandoning Himself to death, He absorbed and dissolved the horror of the curse in His own person. Scripture declares that anyone hanging on a tree embodies the curse. (Deut 21:23)

3:14 <u>This act of Christ</u> released the blessing of Abraham upon the Gentiles! Now we are free to receive the blessing of the Spirit. *(Righteousness by God's faith in the achievement of Christ, and not as a reward to our behavior).*

1 Peter 3:7 Says: A man and his wife are heirs together of the grace of life.
Remember this: "Love is any word or action that flows from within to benefit others, without condition or emotion expecting nothing in return." (Phillip A. Baker)

Love is not contagious, not reluctant but extravagant. Love is selfless, it is not out to take advantage but to give the advantage!

There is nothing you can gain that does not already belong to you in Christ! The world belongs to you! Life and death are yours; in what you now have in this present moment you already possess the future!
Not even death can threaten what you have in life! As much as Christ is inseparably God's own, you are the property of Christ. <u>You are one with Him</u>. Jesus redeemed God's ownership of man. [See Ps 24:1, Mt 13:44, Lk 15].

This is my conviction, no threat whether it be in death or life; be it angelic beings, demon powers or political principalities, nothing is known to us at this time, or even in the unknown future; no dimension of any calculation in time or space, nor any device yet to be invented, has what it takes to separate you from the love of God demonstrated in Christ. Jesus is your ultimate authority. (See Rom 8:38- 39 MB)

"Jesus is the solution to anything contrary to a Graceful, Loving and Peaceful Marriage!"
2 Corinthians 1:20 MB In him the detail of every single promise of God is fulfilled; Jesus is God's yes to your total well being!

Unity Candle Lighting

The unity ceremony symbolizes the joining of the couple and the blending of their two families.

Presentation to the Congregation

To the Groom and Bride: Turn and face the Congregation.

To the Congregation: Ladies and Gentlemen, I present to you:

Mr. & Mrs. ________________________.

Creating Love

Speak the following scriptures as often as needed reminding yourself of your true identity and redeemed innocence. These scriptures are not direct quotations, but rather personalized affirmations based on the word of God. {Taken from my book, Creating the Life of Love}

God's Love for You

God loves me with His undying, never failing, unconditional love and He wants to do me good and make me happy. (Phillip A. Baker)

I am the crown of God's creation, the apple of His eye, marked by His love, and the focus of all His affection. (Phillip A. Baker)

I thank You Lord that Your motive for creating me was Your love, and that I was conceived in love. (Matthew 6:4, MSG)

Father, I thank You, that You found me in Christ before the fall of the world! And that Jesus is Your mind made up about me! You always knew in Your love that You would present me face-to-face before You in blameless innocence. (Ephesians 1:4 MB)

Lord, You have brought me to life using the Word of truth, showing me off as the crown of all Your creation. (James 1:18, MSG)

Father, I thank You for showing me real love. Not that I loved You, but that You loved me and sent Your son as a sacrifice to clear away my sins and the damage they have done to my relationship with You. (1John 4:10, NLT and MSG)

Lord, You have loved me with an everlasting Love, and with unfailing love You have drawn me to Yourself. (Jeremiah 31:3, NLT)

Father, I thank You that I was conceived in love, by Love, for Love, to be loved and to love. (Phillip A. Baker)

Lord I thank You for the good plan You have for me—plans to take care of me, not to abandon me. Plans to give me the future I hope for. (Jeremiah 29:11, MSG)

Father, You told me that You have never quit loving me and never will. According to Your Word, I can expect love, love and more love! (Jeremiah 31:3, MSG)

Freed by Love

Lord, I thank You that Your love for me was so great that You gave Your beloved Son, I realize my oneness in Him, and I am convinced that He is my original life and that His name defines me, in me You have endorse the fact that I am indeed Your offspring. (John 3:16,1:12 MSG, MB)

Lord, I thank You for putting Your love on the line for me—offering Your Son in sacrificial death while I was of no use to You at all. (Romans 5:8, MSG)

Lord, I realized that nothing that I did could distract from Your extravagant love for me; You continued to love me with the exact same intensity. This is how grace rescued me: sin left me dead towards You, yet in that state of deadness and indifference, You made me alive together with Christ. Grace reveals how alive I am now. Praise you Jesus! (Ephesians 2:4, 5, MB)

Lord, I know how dearly You love me because You have given me Your Holy Spirit to fill my heart with Your love. (Romans 5:5, NLT)

Love That Comforts

Father, help me to understand the depth of Christ's Love for me. His love for me was not cautious, but extravagant. He didn't love in order to get something from me, but to give everything of Himself to me. Grace me to love like that. (Ephesians 5:1-2. MSG)

Father, I thank You that through Jesus Christ my Lord Who loves me, You have given me special favor, everlasting comfort and good hope. Thank You for comforting my heart and giving me strength in every good thing I do and say. (2 Thessalonians 2:16, 17, NLT)

Your Love for God

Father I know You love me dearly and I love Your Son and believe He came from You. I thank you for giving me another Comforter Who will never leave me. (John 14:15, 16, NLT)

Lord, You said the person who knows Your commandments of love and allow it to flow from them to others, that's who loves You. And because You first loved them, You will make Yourself plain to them. Jesus, that's me! (John 14:21, MSG)

I am a new creation in Christ and because You first loved me, I am graced to love You. (1John 4:10 KJV)

Lord, I am at rest in Your love, therefore, I trust You to rescue and protect me. When I call upon You, You answer me. Thank You for being with me in trouble, for rescuing and honoring me, and for satisfying me with long life and revealing Jesus to me. (Psalm 91:14-16, NLT)

Lord, thank You for loving me and causing me to inherit wealth and filling my treasuries. (Proverbs 8:21, KJV)

Love in Relationship

Father, because You have made us for each other, male and female, I will leave my father and mother and be firmly bonded to my spouse as one flesh and because You are the Creator of this organic union, I will let no one desecrate it by dividing us. (Matthew 19:5, Message)

Lord, out of respect for You, I will courteously reverence my spouse. (Ephesians 5:21, MSG)

Wife's Confession

As a wife, I will be both understanding, and supportive of my husband in ways I show support for Christ. And as the Church submits to Christ, as He exercises leadership, I will likewise submit to my husband. (Ephesians 5:20-24, MSG)
I will be a gracious wife to my husband, responsive to his needs. My life of holy beauty and inner disposition will captivate him. (1 Peter 3:1-2, MSG)

Husband's Confession

As a husband, I will provide leadership for my wife the way Christ does to His Church. Not by domineering her but cherishing her. (Ephesians 5:23, MSG)
I will go all out in my love for my wife as Christ did for His Church. I will live a life of love marked by giving, not selfishly taking or getting, as Christ's love makes the Church whole. His words evoke her beauty and everything He does and says is designed to bring the best out of her. Ephesians (5:25-28, MSG)

I will not abuse my wife verbally, emotionally or physically, because that would be abusing myself. Instead, I will feed and pamper her as Christ treats the Church, which is a part of His body. (Ephesians 5:29, 30, MSG)

I will be a gracious husband to my wife. I will honor her and delight in her. God's grace has made us equal. Therefore, I will treat her as my equal and my prayers will be heard. (1 Peter 3:7, Message)
I will share my love only with my wife; she is a fountain of blessing to me. Therefore, I will rejoice in her. She is loving and graceful. I am satisfied with the way God made her and will always be captivated by her love. (Proverbs 5:15, 19, NLT)

Love Your Enemies

Lord, my hostility and indifference towards You, did not reduce Your love for me; You saw equal value in me when You exchange the life of Your Son for mine. And by Your grace. I will love those who are not awake to their redeemed identity and innocence in Christ. I will let them bring out the best in me, not the worst. Those who give me a hard time, I will respond to with energies of prayer on their behalf. If someone steals or has stolen something from me, I will gift-wrap my best and present it as a present to them. If someone takes advantage of me, I will use that occasion to practice the servant life. No more tit-for-tat stuff. I will live generously. (Luke 6:27-30, Romans 5:10 MB, MSG)

I chose to live out my God- created identity the way my Father lives toward me- generously and graciously. Even when I am at my worst, He is kind. I will be kind. (Luke 6:35-36, MSG)

 Lord, if my enemy is hungry, I will feed them. If they are thirsty, I will give them something to drink... I will not let evil get the best of me, instead I will conquer evil by doing good. (Romans 12:20-21 NLT)

Loving Others

Lord, I will do Your commandments; I will love others, because You first loved me. By Your grace I will put my life on the line for my friends, because it's the best way to love. (John 15:12-13, MSG)

I will love others with genuine affection and take delight in honoring them. (Romans 12:10, NLT)

As long as life lasts, I will owe a huge debt of love to my neighbor, because love is the essence of the law. (Romans 13:8 MSG, NLT, MB)

I will love my neighbor as I love myself. I will do no wrong to my neighbor, because love is the most complete expression of what the law requires. (Romans 13:9-10, NLT, MB)

Since I have been cleansed from my sins, I will sincerely love my brothers and sisters. I will love them intensely with all my heart. (1 Peter 1:22, NLT)
Father, I will be of one mind and fully sympathetic toward others, loving them with a tender heart and humble mind. I will not repay evil for evil or retaliate when I am treated unkind. Instead, I will pay them back with a blessing, because that is God's will. (1 Peter 3:8-9, NLT)

Because I am in union with Christ, His love flows through me towards others, even though they might have done me wrong. (1 John 2:10, MB)

I love my brothers and sisters; because I have passed from death to eternal life. (1 John 3:14, NLT)

I will not just say I love, but I will really show it by my actions. It is by my actions that prove I am living in the truth, and I will stand confident in the presence of the Lord. (1 John 3:18-19, NLT)

I will continue to love others for love comes from God, and I love because I am born of God and know God, for God is Love. (1 John 4:7-8, NLT)

Lord, because You loved me so much, I will surely love others. You say if I love others, it is proof that You live in me and Your love has been brought to full expression through me. (John 4:11-12, NLT)

When we grasp the revelation of real love [Gods love for us] and embrace it! Knowing that the Holy Spirit completes our every expectation and ignites the love of God within us like an artesian well. Then our hearts will begin to burst forth with His love and begin to splash over into the lives everyone around us.

Love is any word or action that flows from within to benefit others without condition or emotion expecting nothing in return. Even when honor, respect, and appreciation do not return, love still stands and loves because God is love. That revelation was given to me by The Spirit of Love, then it was revealed to me. Jesus is the Word of God. He came from the bosom of the Father and moved into action to benefit humanity without condition or emotion expecting nothing in return. Even when He was not honored, respected or appreciated, He hung on the cross and loved. **"Father forgive them." WOW! What love.**

About the Author

Described by some as—a walking epistle, Phillip Baker was born in Kingston, Jamaica West Indies. He traveled to the United States at the tender age of 12 years old and has been a resident ever since.

While attending World Changers Church International (WCCI) located in College Park, Georgia for over 20 years, Phillip served in many capacities. He was a member of WCCI's and WCNY's ministerial staff, having received training under the leadership of Pastors and founders Dr. Creflo A. Dollar and Taffi L. Dollar. Phillip was granted his ministerial license on May 24, 2004, and his Pastoral Ordination on February 9, 2014. He also served faithfully as a volunteer with the WCCI Youth Ministry for over 10 years.

Phillip's ministry spans over 35 years, which includes preaching the Gospel extensively, and serving in halfway houses, street ministries, youth programs and various other community service opportunities. He has helped to change countless lives through ministering on the love of God and the power that love brings in transforming lives in every situation. A father of two beautiful children, Phillip has been married to his lovely wife, Marva for over 30 years. Phillip and his family currently reside in Powder Springs, Georgia.

For more information about Phillip A. Baker and Phillip Baker Ministries, or for a complete list of books, please contact us at: prevailingword@bellsouth.net, Facebook or on Instagram.

www.ingramcontent.com/pod-product-compliance
Lightning Source LLC
Chambersburg PA
CBHW050713250726

48662CB00002B/992